Money Management For Millennials

5 Steps To Better Managing Your Finances

James Sackey

Copy Right © 2017 James Sackey, 2017

All rights reserved. Without limiting the rights under copyright reserved above, no part of this publication may be reproduced, stored or introduced, into a retrieval system, or transmitted, in any form or by any means (electronic, mechanical, photocopying, recording or otherwise), without the prior written permission of the copyright owner of this book.

ISBN13 978-1978011915
ISBN10 1978011911

Table of Contents

Acknowledgements	v
Introduction	1
Overview Chapter 1: Compounding, Habit, and Discipline	6
The Power of Compounding	6
Discipline	9
Habit	11
Applying It All	13
Overview Chapter 2: Planning Retirement and Financial Goals	15
Laying Out The Plan	15
What Do You Want To Live On	17
Take Action	19
PART I: Building Your Money	**21**
Chapter 1: Saving	23
Out Of Sight Out Of Mind	26
Emergency Fund	26
Retirement Accounts	27
Law Of Saving	30
Chapter 2: Budgeting	32
Knowing Your Budget	32
Living Within Your Means	34

Chapter 3: Avoiding Debt	39
Credit Cards	39
School Loans	42
Auto Loans	46
Avoid Debt	48

PART II: Deploying Your Money — 50

Chapter 4: Invest	52
What To Invest In	52
How To Invest	53
Investment Management	56
Chapter 5: Insurance	58
Three Rules Of Insurance	60
Health	61
Disability	63
Life	65
Other Assets	69
Auto Insurance	71
Wills	72
Conclusion: Pulling It All Together	74
Books to Read	76
Connect with me	78

Acknowledgements

There are really only a few people who have ever actually supported me, my goals, and what I seek in life. I would like to acknowledge my parents, for always supporting me, always having the utmost faith in me and my endeavors. I cannot thank them enough for everything they have done for me. I owe them everything for every bit of who I am and who I aspire to become. I love you.

I acknowledge my closest friends who have always been faithful to me especially during some trying times when many others abandoned, turned on, or otherwise left me. You will always be family to me. I love you.

I have to acknowledge a very special person, the one who encouraged me to write this book despite my personal doubts as to whether or not I was worthy to write it in the first place. You inspire me and mean so much more than I could ever put into words. My Sun, I love you.

Introduction

"If you always do what you have always done, you will always be where you have always been." –
Les Brown

    This book is a personal finance guide aimed at Millennials who want to learn how to better manage their money, retire with a nest-egg they can live off of, or just generally want to have control over their financial well-being. It is meant to be a generalized, no frills guide. Not a comprehensive course in personal finance but more like a crash course intended to tighten up your finances, change your perspective on money management, and get you moving in the right direction.

    I have intentionally written it in a way that should feel relaxed and not overwhelming because typically anything revolving around financial management can be daunting. The chapters and the book in its entirety are intentionally short so that you get the most important information quickly and concisely without losing any flavor for the robustness of what is personal financial management.

    From some perspectives, money is the most important element in anyone's life. They say money isn't everything or that money can't buy happiness. While the intention is pure, statements like these distort the realities of life and the unfortunate world we live in. Money *is* everything and everything *is* money. If you think about it, you can tie almost every single experience in your life back to money in some form or fashion. The friends you have, the schools you attend, the richness for life that you feel, romantic relationships, the clothes you wear, the places you go regularly or vacation, the contacts you have, the food you eat. In one way or another, every aspect of your life is shaped by the money you have, and how much you have or lack thereof.

Every wealthy person is well aware (some even believe it to be a direct link to where you go in life) of the fact that your circle of friends, who you surround yourself with, has one of the biggest impacts on the trajectory of your life, financial or otherwise. Most of us will agree what schools you attend (college, mainly) are based on how much money your parents or you have. Most of us will agree that when you're broke or living paycheck to paycheck, the richness for life is not rich at all. It is likely quite mundane and routine and sometimes – probably most times – you feel like there's no point to get up each morning. Any kind of relationship, romantic or otherwise, will be difficult to create, nurture, and grow in the first place if you can't even leave your house because you are too strapped for cash. How are you going to socialize? Most socializing for people on this planet is oriented around dining out or attending events and activities. But if you have no money to do those things, you simply won't be able to get out and network or meet the love of your life. Obviously, the places you will ever get to see in this world are going to cost you money to travel to and explore them, whether it's a lot of money or not. Money is tied into everything in your life.

I discovered this when I was maybe 16 or 17 years old and the realization of this has only continued to show the truth of it. This is part of the reason I decided at that time to become as versed in matters of money as I possibly could. I wanted to know *everything* about money – from personal to business to investing, on all levels.

I have never worked for a big box financial firm – and I never will. Around the same time I decided to start learning about money, I also discovered some of the horrible ways in which big businesses and the people who run them – in particular, those who play the biggest roles in the financial industry – have caused irreparable damage to so many others; economically and emotionally. It sowed the seeds of a deep disdain toward the financial services industry for me.

Because of this, I have taken it upon myself to always be willing to offer as much advice and help people as much as I can in money matters and why my philosophy, methodology, and approach is very different from that of a usual financial professional. It is also why I urge people, most of the time, to avoid financial professionals as much as possible. The industry has been very clever to shroud itself in mystery and the idea that what financial professionals do is some kind of wizardry reserved only for the smartest people on the planet. That no normal human being can possibly comprehend what takes place on Wall Street or in financial markets across the globe.

Let me clarify that the financial services industry is not a "helping" industry, so to speak. It is a *sales* industry. No different from car sales, retail clothing sales, or anything else where the majority of salaries paid to its agents comes from commission. That is why financial professionals tend to make so much money – their pay is directly tied to how much they *sell* to consumers. The conflict of interest should be clear. In fact, there was a book written in 1940 by a guy named Fred Schwed highlighting that very conflict called *Where Are All The Customers' Yachts*. The title of the book is derived from the comment of a New York tourist who, when shown the East River was told "there are all the great Wall Street brokers yachts", to which the tourist replied, "where are all the customers' yachts?" I don't know about you, but I have never met anyone who, through the advice of their financial advisor, retired any earlier or wealthier than anyone else who simply saves money regularly, lives within their means, and doesn't have a financial advisor.

It is my intent to give you this guide to shed light on many of the factors and elements of personal financial management and that, by the end of it, you will be equipped with the knowledge and tools to manage your finances like a champ. So that, one day, you won't have to worry about money ever again.

This book begins with two overview chapters intended to set the tone. The first is more of a mindset you need to adopt if you are ever going to get your money situation figured out. This mindset can be used in all other areas of your life, however, and I strongly encourage you use it. It will quite literally change your life. Give it a try.

The second talks more about numbers and goals you need to figure out. But don't worry, it's really nothing too complicated. The overview chapters are essentially what you *need* to get to the end; the five main subsequent chapters are the *how* you will get there.

Let us begin.

Overview Chapter 1: Compounding, Discipline, and Habit

"You can only fight the way you practice." –
Miyamoto Musashi

The Power of Compounding

Compounding is the most powerful force known to man. Albert Einstein knew it. Warren Buffett knows it. And now you know it. But I want you to *understand* it. The best way to understand is through relative example. Let's take a very simple compound interest example.

Let's say an investment returns you 8% annually. That means with $1,000 invested, by the end of the year it'll return you $80 (8% of $1,000 is $80). That's nice. But it isn't anything really worth chatting to your friends about. But over time, that 8% profit reinvested each year, at the same rate of interest return, can add up on itself. Extend that 1 year to 30 years. Now, your $1,000 becomes $10,063 – over 10 times your original investment. Scale that math up by putting another zero in and making your beginning investment $10,000. $10,000 becomes $100,000+, all from a single investment and the power of compounding interest. It becomes interest on interest.

This is not an arithmetic (simple) return, where you calculate for an $80 profit each year, add it up, and that's your final return – as in $80 x 30 years = $2,400 + your original $1,000 for a total of $3,400.

Keep in mind, if you are reinvesting *all* of your profits each year (and assuming your investment always goes up in value, which is not reality but for the sake of simplicity we'll assume so), the dollar amount of your reinvestment is growing. 8% of $1,000 is $80 but 8% of $1,500 is $120 and 8% of $3,000 is $240 – each of those, by the way, is reinvested each time. You need to find the *compounded* return. To calculate that, you start with $1,000 multiply it by 1 plus the rate (1.08 in this case) and raise the 1.08 to the power of however many years you want to calculate (30 in this case). So the calculation looks like this: 1000 x (1.08^30) = 10,063. If you wanted to change the rate to, say, 11%, the formula would simply be: 1000 x (1.11^30) = 22,892. What a difference 3% can make, right? Increase the rate just 3% and the end number is more than double. *That* is the exact concept described above – the effect of compounding. The money, the profit, adds up on itself exponentially.

There's a story about Benjamin Franklin that reflects the power of compounding. When Franklin died in 1790, he left a gift of $5,000 to Boston and Philadelphia, each. The money was to be invested and paid out at100 years and 200 years after the date of the gift. After 100 years, each city was allowed to withdraw $500,000 for public works projects. After 200 years, in 1991, they received the balance – which had compounded to approximately $20 million for each city. Franklin's example teaches all of us, in a dramatic way, the power of compounding. Franklin himself has been quoted saying, "Money makes money. And the money that money makes, makes money."

There is another, more abstract example of the power of compounding in the form of an experiment. This experiment was conducted by a physicist in San Francisco adapted from a previous experiment first conducted by a man named Lorne Whitehead in the 1980s. The physicist setup dominoes made out of plywood where each one was 50% larger to the subsequent domino. He began with a domino in size of a mere 2 inches – a regular size playing domino. The last domino was just less than 3 feet tall. As you might imagine, it doesn't take much beyond a simple flick of the finger to knock over a 2 inch domino. But the resulting force, compounded, was enough to knock over an almost 3 ft. tall domino – substantially larger than the beginning domino.

Take this example further and continue to scale the proverbial dominos larger and larger. By the 10th domino, it's around 6 ft. tall. By the 18th domino, approximately 186 ft. By the 23rd domino, you're over the Eiffel Tower. By the 31st, you're taller than Mount Everest (which is around 29,000 ft.) by about 3,000 ft. It is almost unimaginable. This is the power of compounding. Something can start off so small and unimpressive but, over time and compounding, can become massive and beyond comprehension.

But what about compounding in other areas of life? I can tell you that compounding exists, quite literally, in every facet of your life in ways that you haven't realized, let alone noticed. In fact, your life is made up entirely of compounding, just in the form of what is better labeled as habit. But before we get to the element of habit it is necessary to discuss what precedes habit and that is discipline.

Discipline

Everyone has heard of Michael Phelps. He is the most decorated Olympian in history, both as an Olympian and in his respective sport as a swimmer. At only 31 years old, he had attended 5 Olympic Games where he won 28 gold medals, 3 silver medals, and 2 bronze medals. Phelps is renowned for his highly focused training regimen in which he was able to form the foundation for his success in the pool – that foundation for success was built using discipline.

Phelps' training consisted of a 7-day week, as opposed to the 5-day week that most other swimmers and athletes use. He made it a personal goal to make sure he was in the pool swimming every single day. Not only did he swim every day, he made sure to spend between 3 to 5 hours doing so. This equated to swimming 70,000 to 100,000 yards, *each* day. This is the caliber of training and discipline it takes to become great. This is what it takes to become disciplined – working at it every single day, without cease.

Discipline is what is required to form and develop habit – it is the prerequisite. I assure you, you will need to use some serious discipline if you are to start managing your money better because right now, it's safe to assume, you have poor money habits and they are stifling your ability to have money and they keep you living paycheck to paycheck. However, discipline is not necessarily something you have to practice every day, *forever*. Rather, discipline need only be practiced for just long enough to become habitual.

Gary Keller, author of *The One Thing: The Surprisingly Simple Truth behind Extraordinary Results*, writes "success is actually a short race – a sprint fueled by discipline just long enough for habit to kick in and take over." But how long is long enough? Well, statistically speaking, researchers have concluded it takes roughly two months (66 days) to form a habit. Therefore, you need enough discipline to last you around two months to turn it into a habit. But honestly, you simply need as much discipline until it becomes habit. There is no set amount of days because everyone is different.

When you use discipline at this high level – the level to affect change – you will have to give up on some things. You will have to make sacrifices. Michael Phelps' swimming and sleeping so many hours each day (he slept around 11 hours a day to recover) clearly suggests when you're focused and maintaining discipline, you don't have much time for anything else. So the question becomes: what are you willing to sacrifice in order to become stronger financially? What will you give up? Morning coffees that cost you $5? Expensive nights out on the town binging on alcohol and good times? Unnecessary living space in the upscale part of town that really does you no good? The amount of time (or how much money you spend, rather) when you hang out with friends? What is it worth to you to have not only peace of mind that your finances are in order and strong but that you will, eventually, have all of the things you want in life?

If you can focus on the long-term and maintain your discipline to manage your money better and adhere to what I will teach you throughout this book enough to build habit, you will be successful. I guarantee it.

Habit

An adapted quote I often remind myself of or tell others is "show me your habits, I'll show you your life." Habit makes up your entire life. It is your daily routine. It is what you typically resort to when your emotions come into play in any given situation. Every bit of habit adds up. Just like we saw with compounding interest and the dominoes, how small amounts of something can add up on itself to monumental amounts of something. Have you ever asked yourself "how did I end up here?" or "how did I get so far off track?" The answer is habit. You are where you are because of the choices you've made that turned into habit or routine and it evolved and escalated into something much bigger than you realized it would without you noticing until it was probably too late.

Think about saving $5 a day. That's a tiny amount of money, right? Every day? No problem. Now calculate saving $5 every single day for 5 years. What do you get? $9,125. That's the power of habit and how small steps in one direction, *over time*, can add up tremendously. It is known by behavioral scientists and psychologists that once we get going in a given direction, we tend to continue in that direction (look up Stanley Milgram's obedience to authority experiment). That's why sometimes in life it feels like we're on a losing streak, like we just can't get anything right. Or perhaps you experience a winning streak when nothing can seemingly go wrong for you. We begin down a path and it becomes easy to continue it. It can also bring about changes in other areas of our lives and create other habits.

In 1987, Paul O'Neil took over as CEO of Alcoa. His first day was somewhat of a notorious one because he walked into a meeting of shareholders, analysts, and journalists and claimed his number one focus for the company was going to be worker safety – far flung from the usual talk of a new CEO on topics like profit margins, sales, marketing and the like.

O'Neil became famous as he was able to turn the company around in such a short time. Within a year, company profits hit a record high. By the time he had retired 13 years later in 2000, net profits were 5 times larger than when he arrived, and market capitalization (value of the company) had risen by $27 billion.

The reason the company saw such a dramatic change was because O'Neil's creation of a company culture that habitually focused on worker safety brought about other habits such as employees recommending other business improvements that would have otherwise received no attention. It fostered better communication throughout the organization, which inevitably resulted in higher profits. The takeaway here is that habit adds up. It compounds and it is contagious in more ways than one. "People do not decide their futures, they decide their habits and their habits decide their futures." – F.M. Alexander.

Applying It All

Once you have exercised your ability to stay focused and disciplined enough to form the habit of managing your money better by using it in smarter ways and cutting out the unnecessary, you will then be on autopilot, essentially. It will become habit for you to cut your spending and save, to pay off debts quickly, invest your savings, to stay on top of your bills or cut them down, and live within your means. You won't have to consciously think about your spending and the clothes you bought yesterday, or what unexpected doctor bill is coming up next, or if you have enough money for rent. You'll know what to do or it'll already be taken care of. Achieving this level of unconscious money management will eventually ease the pressure and eliminate stresses you have toward money, which will then lead to a much happier state of being. That is the goal - the real goal. Being in a state of happiness and satisfaction in life should be where you seek to get. Managing your money well is simply the strategy employed to get there.

Applying all of these things is straightforward. Now that you understand how compounding works and how discipline evolves into habit and what it can lead to, you have to **take action** and begin using them. As you read through this book, you will begin to see exactly how to do just that – what options and tools you have available, where to put your money, how to save, how to spend effectively, but most of all, how to take back control of your life through stronger management of your money.

You need to be very aware though of just what it's going to take from you in order to get your finances straight. It will take a lot of time, willpower, focus, and commitment, among the other attributed character traits outlined in this chapter. Smart financial management takes the long-term outlook. Your goals are big. Or maybe they are more modest. Either way, you must approach this with both a long-term outlook and an outlook focused on inches, days, weeks, and months. Little by little, each day, you will work and progress toward each of your goals – building, cutting, and adding to your finances in some of the smallest of ways that will pay off big many years down the road.

A favored writer of mine, Ryan Holiday, tells of a friend of his who teaches martial arts. The teacher explained to him that practicing martial arts is like sweeping the floor. You cannot simply sweep the floor one time and it stays clean forever. It is something you have to do *every single day*.

Overview Chapter 2: Planning Retirement and Financial Goals

"All of us are self-made. But only the successful will admit it." – Les Brown

Laying Out The Plan

Like any great undertaking, a well thought out and deliberate plan for managing your finances is fully necessary. In *The Art of War*, Sun Tzu said "every battle is won before it is ever fought" – it's all in the preparation. With that in mind, you need to start figuring out what you want to see in your retirement years. There are several important questions you need to ask yourself in order to determine how to setup your financial plan and what steps you need to take to ensure that you reach your retirement goals.

When planning, I have always found it easier to start at the end and work backward. Or else begin with a broad picture in mind of what you want and then shrink it down several levels until you get to the level you are currently at. This latter method is also known as *effectuation* and can be very useful and practical to form your plan with sound strategy.

Effectuation is a way of thinking – an approach – that deals with uncertainty. Most people think in terms of the opposite, which would be *causation*. Let me illustrate the difference. Causation says "if I can predict the future, I can control it", whereas effectuation says, "if I can control the future, I need not predict it." For example, think of a chef cooking a meal. By causation, the client chooses a menu in advance and the chef prepares this menu by looking for the right ingredients and following the recipes to make the dishes. In the effectual process, the client would not ask for a specific menu, but he asks the chef to make something with the ingredients available. The chef chooses one of the many different meals he is able to make with the available ingredients. The key difference with effectuation is that you act using what you have at your disposal right now; what you know; and who you know.

In either method (effectuation or starting at the end at working backward), you need to begin planning *right now* because retirement comes much quicker than anyone ever thinks. Especially when you consider there will literally be thousands of distractions and derailments and unexpected challenges that will inevitably pop up throughout the rest of your life. It's important to remain flexible in your planning and to form a plan that can be adapted for several instances of change – effective planning encompasses broad consideration and objective thought not a narrow perspective of what you simply *want* to happen.

The main thing to remember though is once you have created your plan and start down the path of your plan to *stay with it*! Consistency is key in executing any plan. Lack of consistency is why people don't lose weight and then quit after only 3 weeks of working out – not enough time was committed. It's a process. It will be slow. You may second guess the plan. You might even think the plan is flawed somewhere. But you have to remain steadfast and believe that it is right and that it will eventually put you in a strong financial position later in life. Remember the vision you created for yourself. The finish line. You will get there before you know it.

What Do You Want To Live On

A good place to start in your planning for retirement is to determine what you want to live on – what kind of lifestyle you want. We can make this easy. Do you want to live on $50,000 a year? $100,000? Maybe $500,000 or more? Whatever the number is, whatever lifestyle you want to maintain, will give you the number your plan will shoot for. Once you have figured out these questions, you will begin to see the end – the end of your work life and the start of your retirement.

Let's work this by example. We'll use a little bit of math to gain a better perspective of how simple it is to begin planning retirement – don't worry, the math is easy enough.

Let's assume you decide you want to live on $100,000 a year or about $8,300 a month (before taxes). Assuming you were to retire around 65 (most people don't retire at 59 anymore; they have tended to work longer or even retire somewhat early and then reenter the workforce). Life expectancy varies of course, but we'll further assume you'll live to the ripe old age 85 years old. That's 20 years in retirement (easy math so far, right?). With the goal of living on $100,000 a year, for a whole 20 years, that means your financial plan, your budget, saving, and investments between now and retirement will need to amass to about $2 million. Not too shabby but definitely a couple of pretty pennies.

How are you going to get there?

Therein lays the golden question. Therein lays the need for an effective budget and savings plan. Continuing our simple math, if you're 25 years old now (if not, adjust accordingly), that means you have about 40 years to build up that 2 million bucks; which amounts to $50,000 built up *each* year. That's tough for anyone with an average salary and common obligations such as rent, car note, et cetera. That is why it's critical to start living on less and start saving *right now*.

I want to make a point here to illustrate that you don't necessarily have to save $50,000 every single year for 40 years to hit your $2 million mark – considering the aim of this book and who its intended for, the odds of you attaining that level of money each and every year is virtually impossible (beyond the lottery or some unexpected, large inheritance, obviously).

Let me provide a more realistic example of how it's feasible to build that much money over your life time using one particular tool I explained to you earlier. Remember how compounding works and how, over time, it can amount to drastically large sums. Let's say you are able to save $2,000 a month, on average, each year. That's $24,000 a year. Let's further assume you invest every dollar of that savings and it returns you a rate of 12% a year (just higher than the average historic rate of return of the U.S. stock market). Over 40 years that means your yearly $24,000 will have amassed into $2,233,223 – just north of your $2M goal. (the calculation is: $24,000 x (1.12^40) = $2,233,223)

Now, you have to take into account several variable factors that could drastically change that final number. Some such factors are taxes, your monthly savings rate and salary, market returns, and inflation, to name a few. Because of the long length of time in this calculation, the numbers are very sensitive. For instance, if the investment returns on your money is increased by just one percent to 13%, the final number becomes $3,186,757, a difference of $953,534 from the original $2 million number. If you increase savings a mere $500 a month to $2,500 and keep the original 12% returns, the final number becomes $2,791,529, a difference of $558,305. As you can see, small changes add up. Witness the power of compounding yet again.

Although there are many factors that could affect your money between now and retirement, the example above should help to put your mind at ease a bit and provide a much more realistic context of how you might be able to achieve your financial goals. Even if they *are* lofty.

Take Action

Up to this point, I have laid out an outline of what kind of approach you need to take toward building a financial plan for yourself and how to figure out your end goal and work backward to determine where you need to start. But that is only half of the coin. In life there are always two sides of a coin in any situation. In this case, the first is *knowing* something while the second is *doing* something with the knowledge. The following chapters will be focused on the latter half of that coin – the doing. This is where we'll get into the meat of personal financial management and you can get yourself working to your goals but more importantly get your money working *for you* and less of the other way around.

PART I: Building Your Money

You simply cannot make progress toward your financial goals without having any money in the first place. So, we need to first focus on you building it up. Hopefully, you are already employed or have some stream of income. If not, focus on getting that in place first and foremost.

You need to build your money but in order to do that you need to be able to control it. The strategy here is going to be making smart decisions to *control* your money. Once you gain control over your money, you can then wield it to make you *more* money. You will also need to protect your money. That will be the focus of Part II. So when you read through these next three chapters, keep in mind the goal is to learn how to control your money, or rather control yourself because these are really matters of self-control.

Chapter 1: Saving

"If you do what is hard, your life will be easy. If you do what is easy, your life will be hard." – Les Brown

There is a reason this is the first main chapter. Saving is by far the most important piece of your financial well-being. It is one of the many key factors that separate the masses from the top 1%. It is what separates the haves and the have not's. It is what separates the financially successful to those who will never have even a couple hundred bucks they don't absolutely need. It is also the very first step you need to take if you ever hope to retire; be able to avoid the inevitable and unexpected pitfalls of life; or be so fortunate as to invest money in any returning asset.

My goal is to help you build yourself a focused financial plan that will get you moving in the right direction toward your goals and get you out of the financial struggle you're in. It starts with saving. It starts with the right mindset as well. There is a very simple tenet you must follow now, religiously. Pay very close attention here.

You Must Pay Yourself FIRST.

Read that again. It's that important.

It is that important because that is the exact point where the majority of people miss the mark entirely in the management of their money. Like everyone else, you have most likely been taught to pay all your bills and expenses first and then whatever is left is your savings. You always pay everyone else first and then maybe transfer the remaining few dollars to your savings if there's anything left.

This method is dead WRONG and the majority of people believe otherwise. Lo and behold, the majority of people are broke. Is it any wonder then that this mentality doesn't foster financial growth? Paying everyone else and then yourself last does not yield more money in your bank account. Period.

We must adopt a new policy with our money: You pay yourself first (I said it again in case you didn't read it twice the first time). You are your first creditor. You are your first expense. You must think about saving as if it were any other recurring bill each month. You shave off a piece of your income every month or every paycheck in the amount of at least 10%. Once you begin doing this regularly, you will put yourself and your finances 10, 20, 30 times ahead of the majority of people in this country and the rest of the world. The average amount of money saved annually by Americans floats between 4% and 6% of their salary. Meaning, for every $100 of after-tax income, they save around $5. You will **not** be in that statistic anymore. In fact, if you really want to supercharge your money and savings, you should be saving every dollar you make beyond your regular monthly expenses on necessities.

For example, if your monthly expenses such as rent, car note, groceries, etc. comes out to something like $1,200 and your income is $2,000, you only spend $1,200 that month. That's it. Not a dime more.

You bank the remaining $800. That's what a financially savvy person would do. That is what you will do.

If you wonder whether or not I practice what I preach, let me dispel the notion. At the time of this writing, I owe money to the state I live in, my best friends, the colleges I went to as well as the Federal government, and my car is in dire need of maintenance and repairs (I had no air conditioning the entire Summer and I live in Texas). Let me be the first to tell you; it has been a more than rough year this year in many aspects but financially in particular. It happens. Yet, I *still* will pay myself before paying everyone else. It is the only way to get ahead. It is the only way to ensure my survival financially. And I assure you, all of those I owe money to will attest to such debts – they are not made up. My focus will be aimed at rebuilding some savings first and then to begin paying down everything I owe second. I have always been able to save between 1/3 and up to half of my income, each month. I know you can as well. But only if you are prepared to make sacrifices and take control of yourself, your finances, and your life.

Keep in mind everything you have read already in the first overview chapter because getting your finances in order and your life on track will not happen in any short time. It will take a lot of time, will, focus, patience, discipline, and commitment, like all things in life worth having.

Out of Sight, Out of Mind

A trick to saving more of your income is to divert your savings into an account that is not your regular checking out (specifically one that is not attached to any debit card or online/mobile transfer; the further you are from accessing, it the better). There are a couple ways of doing this. Retirement accounts are one way but I will address those in greater detail in a moment. Another way you can begin diverting money before you see it is to ask your employer to divert the money for you directly into your savings account. Many employers (particularly those who offer direct deposit) offer the ability to divert any amount of your paycheck to more than one account even before you see it in your checking account. This way, when your check hits your bank account and you look at it, your mind automatically believes this is the only amount of money you have to spend. If you have already started mapping out your finances using what I have illustrated and you are on point already, the amount left in your bank account should be just enough to cover your regularly occurring monthly bills.

Emergency Fund

There are many goals and objectives to save for. What should be the first is known as an emergency fund. If you have never heard of an emergency fund don't worry, most young people have not either. An emergency fund, or "e-fund", is meant for emergencies, as its name implies. That's like when you lose your job. Or your car breaks down unexpectedly and you need a tow and some repairs. Or you get hurt and your insurance is either non-existent or somehow isn't fully covering you or any other extenuating circumstances that may befall you.

The e-fund is generally meant to cover any periods of unemployment so you can still manage to pay your regular bills each month. This savings account is tough to build because, as a rule of thumb, it needs to equal 3 to 9 months of your regular bills – 3 if you can easily find another, equal paying job, 9 if it will be difficult to find a new job with equal pay. So if your regular expenses each month come to $1,800 and your job/income is moderately hard to replace, you want to have 6 months' expenses saved in the e-fund, or about $10,800 in this example. Your e-fund is not to be touched – you do not with draw from it or invest with it. It is meant to be your cash flow in the event you lose your normal cash flow so no playing with that account.

Don't be daunted by the large amount of savings the e-fund requires. No one said you had to build it immediately. But **do not** ignore it. Remember compounding; things add up over time. Small amounts of money diverted and left alone add up (remember the $5 coffee). Work at it. Be disciplined. Be habitual. You will get there.

Retirement Accounts

Another area you definitely want to divert a portion of your income to is any retirement accounts available to you. These include: Defined

Contribution Plan (401k), Individual Retirement Account (IRA), and Simplified-Employee Pension (SEP, for the self-employed), to name a few. You should be utilizing these types of accounts, particularly if your employer offers 401(k) matching. Matching means they contribute as much money as you do, up to an annual limit – Congress changes that limit from time to time so be sure to check what the current laws are. I highly encourage you to take advantage of your employer's 401(k) program, especially for the matching because it is the only free money in life (yes, there is actually a free lunch).

If you don't know what a 401(k) retirement account is, it is simply a tax-deferred savings account. The "401(k)" part references the U.S. tax code. "Tax-deferred" means that you don't pay taxes on the money contributed to the account until you withdraw that money during retirement – so instead of paying taxes right now, as you do on the rest of your paycheck, you pay them later once you retire and start withdrawing from the account. The idea is that during your prime working years, which are between 25 and 50, you will likely be in a higher tax bracket than when you retire (since you won't have any actual workforce-related income during retirement).

Another option for saving money specifically for retirement is the IRA. There are two types of IRA's: A regular IRA and a Roth IRA. I will highlight the main differences.

In a regular IRA, the account is also tax-deferred (pay taxes later). There is no income limit but you must begin withdrawing from the account when you turn 70 ½. You cannot withdraw before 59 ½ without a sizeable penalty. This type makes the most sense if, like with a 401(k), you will be in the same or a lower tax bracket upon retirement.

In a Roth IRA, the account is tax-exempt (meaning you pay the taxes upfront) so when you begin withdrawing from the account in retirement, you will not be hit with any taxes. There is an income limit and it changes from time to time, but usually the limit is around $95,000 if you file *Single* on your taxes. There is no age limit or forced withdrawal. Also, first-time home buyers can withdraw up to $10,000 in profits penalty-free and tax-free after the money has been in the account for at least 5 years. This type of IRA makes the most sense if you will be in a higher tax-bracket upon retiring.

There are other options as far as retirement accounts, like if you're self-employed, or work for the government but the ones I have highlighted here are suited to the majority. If you are not in the majority, consider looking into other options for retirement account saving as there can be some very useful methods of saving for retirement depending on your situation. That being said, the majority should aim to use as many methods of saving as possible. The order in which you save is also important to consider. Generally, you want to fund your 401(k) first because it has a maximum and its free money if your employer matches. Followed by your e-fund or regular savings (they can be the same, if you so choose). After that, fund your IRA to its maximum. Now, the order depends, of course, on your specific situation as some priorities may be more pressing than others at different times but in general you want to build all of these accounts simultaneously – little by little, in each account.

However, if a major goal of yours is to, say, pay down a large, high-interest debt or save for a house, then you have to incorporate that *into* your saving. Notice I said "into", not "instead of". Because you pay yourself first, as we now know. You cannot forgo saving in lieu of paying a bill, even if it's a goal to do so. You simply do both at the same time, in whatever amount you can afford. No matter how small it is. Remember: this is also a game of inches and days. You won't always use a sledge hammer. Sometimes you have to use a pick axe.

Law of Saving

Saving a portion of income regularly should be law. It *is* law, now. In fact, George S. Clason, author of one of the most powerful classics of financial literature ever, *The Richest Man In Babylon*, told of a very wealthy man by the name of Arkad who wrote the 5 laws of money several millennium ago. The very 1st law read "Gold cometh gladly and in increasing quantity to any man who will put by not less than one-tenth of his earnings to create an estate for his future and that of his family."

You now understand the first step in financial management. Save.

Chapter 2: Budgeting

"If it doesn't challenge you, it won't change you." –
Unknown

Know Your Budget

You probably have never lived on a budget. Likely, the word is probably foreign to you – something you only hear maybe at your job. Well now it is about to become second nature for you because using a budget is absolutely critical to your financial success. You must know your budget. But before you know your budget, you must first learn *what* a budget is.

A budget is an accounting of your financial expenses and liabilities. A spreadsheet, in a sense, that shows all of the things that require your hard earned money on a regular basis. A budget shows the details of where your money needs to go in order for you to survive and satisfy your means of living. It is of the utmost importance to know and thoroughly understand where your money goes on a regular basis. Remember that your routines and habits add up to monumental sums and that if they are left unbridled and free to run, they can take you to terrible places you won't even recognize and leave you wondering how you could have ever ended up there.

That is what a budget is – a check against your plans for the use of money. It tells you where your money needs to go.

In the case of *your* budget, it is slightly different in that it is unique. It is tailor-made just for you. It details and accounts for your obligations and tells where your money needs to go, based on your lifestyle.

As such, you need to put pen to paper and write up your monthly budget. Your budget should contain the following:
- Mortgage/Rent
- Car Note (if applicable)
- Phone/TV
- Utilities
- Insurance
- Groceries

The list above is not exhaustive but shows the minimum of what should be on any budget because there are essentials to living, particularly in any developed country such as the United States. Yours may require more items, but it's likely those items are not necessity to sustaining life or a general well-being. That does not mean those items are unnecessary or superfluous. It simply means that those are items unique to you as an individual and, likely, they are items that can be altered and controlled. The others listed above cannot be altered much.

This is the difference between an expense and a liability in accounting. A liability is an item that a business owes to a creditor or some good or service the business has received but has not yet paid for – it is usually a long-term obligation. An expense is basically a cost of operating – short-term, typically. Expenses are the enemy in the majority of budgets. They are parasitic – they drain the money from your bank account over time without you really noticing it.

Your budget should contain all of your regular obligations incurred on a monthly (weekly, quarterly, or annual) basis. If you know it needs to be paid for in a given month, it should be marked on your budget. Simple as that. This includes items that vary as well – the expenses. Items like entertainment, dining out, trips, splurge items, whatever. These too should be marked and planned for ahead of time in the budget and accounted for. One caveat: budget for your obligations and expenses but **do not exceed the budgeted amount**. That is a rule for spending control. This is the essence of a budget – a set amount you can spend on an item. If you want to allow yourself $100 a month to eat at a fancy restaurant, that's fine. Just budget for it. Then stay within the budgeted amount. Don't spend $101 or anything beyond your budget. This way, you stay in control of your money and know where it's all going.

Know your budget. Live your budget.

Live Within Your Means

The vast majority of people simply do not live within their means and tend to dramatically overspend, most of the time without being aware of it and usually through some form of credit extended to them. This is usually in the form of a car or home that is honestly too costly for their income to sustain, in addition to their other obligations and expenses of their chosen lifestyle. Make no mistake either, lifestyle is certainly a choice – it is based almost exclusively on pride, on ego. And ego is the enemy.

There are no hard and fast rules but a good rule of thumb for some bigger ticket items most of us have is that your home should not be 50% of your income. It should be maybe 33% or less. A car should definitely not take up more than 15%. Even with those limits in place, in what would be a realistic example, it's still pushing it. If you make $3,000 a month and your apartment costs you $1,000 (33% of income) in rent and your car note runs about $450 (15% of income), they total $1,450 or about 48% of your income. While you're doing alright, remember that you have to add in all the other costs of living your lifestyle with the remaining half of your money. Remember the first rule in the book – you have to be saving regularly on top of all that!

In the example, you would shave off $300 (10% of income) in the beginning so you would really start off with $2,700 in monthly income, not the full $3,000. After your rent and car note, you have $1,250 remaining (less than half your money) to be spent on whatever other obligations are within your budget. Or added to your savings. That would be phenomenal. But here again, remember, you should be aiming to fund several savings accounts in order to protect your retirement nest-egg that will come due at some point toward the end of your life and its meant to sustain you until you die. The question is: will you be prepared for it?

A person makes $100,000 a year and lives on $110,000 and then wonders why they have no money. It is mind-blowing. They survive on outsized credit, exacerbated by late fees and interest charges, and live paycheck to paycheck with no idea of how their bank account is dwindling. All the while adding insurmountable stress and hardship to their lives, straining relationships with loved ones, feeling overworked and underpaid, like they will never be free of their financial burdens as they relentlessly pile up. There again, an example of compounding and (poor) habits.

This is why knowing your budget and living within your means is so important. If you have both, you will eliminate all of these obstacles and the draining feelings of stress and inadequacy that stem from financial hardship. Instead you will keep yourself sane and financially healthy.

How do you live within your means? Maintain a sensible budget and don't exceed it. Live in a place that you can afford, not one that boosts your ego yet takes half of your income. Buy a car you can afford, not one that's big, fast, or pretty and takes up a quarter of your income. Eat at home. Buy off-brand or on sale clothing, or even slightly used. Avoid driving everyday and carpool instead or take mass transportation or combine your trips. Pay your bills on time, every time, and avoid late fees and interest charges. One very powerful tactic I always tell people (and have repeated in this book) is to only have enough money in your bank account to pay the bills due on your budget, the ones that are regular obligations and necessity. Want more? Cut up your credit cards. Pay in full as much as you can on all of your purchases. Save 20% of your income. Save more than 20%, if you can. Then you'll really see your money grow.

Grant Sabatier was able to make himself a millionaire within just 6 years – by the time he reached 30 years old. He is a millennial. In fact, CNBC has dubbed him the "Millennial Millionaire". Sabatier wrote a very interesting article for Business Insider in 2017 describing what it took to get there. The steps he took were entirely focused on living within his means, intense saving, and investing the money he built up.

"Most people didn't get it", says Sabatier. People around him would ask, "You save 80% of your income? You have a six-figure income so shouldn't you have a nice car? I'm sorry, Grant, but why do you live in such a crappy apartment when you make so much money?" But Sabatier never let any of this bother him. He knew that in order to retire properly and become financially independent, he needed to do all the things everyone else wouldn't: sacrifice, in addition to being patient, focused, and disciplined about managing his money (see quote at beginning of chapter).

According to research Sabatier conducted, he found that the average American spends 70% of their money on housing, transportation, and food and that if he could cut down his spending on these to maybe

25%, he could save the rest and take bigger steps to retiring early. Sabatier says his savings rate jumped to 40% and was sometimes as high as 80% while fast tracking himself to financial independence. To put that into some perspective for you, I personally have friends whose finances I have analyzed and found that they could be saving $15,000 to $30,000 a year and they have zero savings at all and this equates to maybe 50% or less of their income.

The money Sabatier saved from cutting back came out to an additional $13,000 a year, which he ultimately invested in retirement accounts that compounded into over $100,000 in just a few short years. He plans to continue to let the money grow for the next 20 years of life.

You now understand the second step in financial management. Budget.

Chapter 3: Avoid Debt

"Are you mentally tough enough to handle the criticism you are going to get on your way to getting rich?" – Steven Siebold

Credit Cards

One of the most infamous financial tools offered to consumers: the credit card. First introduced as a means of floating your finances in between paychecks, that evolved into a status statement and then a method to gain back "rewards" for frequent flyers on travel mileage that could be redeemed for dollars to be freely spent on other products. Cash back incentives for spending on big ticket items with your credit card. "Buy that shiny new toy now, we'll figure out the payment later, Mr. Consumer." What's not to love?

Fast-forward to the generation of late Gen-X'ers and Millennials; now, the infamous credit card is understood by some to be an unforgiving, one-way ticket to financial death via bleeding out that will simply never clot. It is passed off these days as a means to build your precious credit history in your younger years so you can buy a mortgage later in life like a real adult or get into an overpriced luxury vehicle, but not before you're graciously hired in a job in a field that you actually majored in college.

Sounds like a dream from your parents' time.

That's exactly why we need to address the matter of debt in the form of a credit card at this stage – because subtle nightmares masquerading as dreams can be very fatal.

Remember in the previous chapter that living beyond our means is one of the most major reasons so many people remain broke, despite even having powerful positions in their careers, corner offices, and above-average salaries. A credit card builds your credit history. Sure. As do many other things. But it is also a window-dressed gateway down a most slippery slope if you are not extremely careful using such an instrument.

Introductory rates, cash back, travel incentives, rewards at special venues and restaurants. Credit card companies have a big bag of goodies for anyone willing enough to listen to their pitch – it's easy to sell crack to kids. It takes strength to not be lured into a credit card application with so many incentives and access to more cash than you currently have in your bank account, especially when these companies bombard your mailbox with offer, after offer, after offer. Only those who have already been down the path of credit card debt are fully aware of this and the financially fatal consequences of poor impulse control, not living on a budget, and inconsistent income.

Credit card debt can absolutely ruin your life.

Remember what you've learned about compounding, habit and routines – they can lead to vast sums very quickly without you noticing until you finally one day you catch yourself thinking: how did I end up here? How could I have let things get so far out of control?

The same applies to credit card debt, times ten.

Credit cards give you unbridled access to live right beyond your means. Do not fall for it. Remember: pay in full, if you can. If not, then you can't afford it. Period.

If you want to build your credit, there are other means of doing so. Having an apartment in your name and paying the rent builds your credit. Having a car note, even with a co-signer, builds your credit. Just make sure to never miss a payment because it will hurt both their and your credit scores. Another option you can take is to go see a personal banker at your bank and ask to take out a secured loan. A secured loan, basically, is a loan granted to you in an amount of cash that you already have in your bank account (hence "secured"). Sounds backwards, I know; you're getting a loan for an amount you already actually have. The point is not to extend actual "credit" to you but to build your credit history in an absolutely safe way. You get the opportunity to make payments, with an interest rate (it's very, very small interest), and show that you can be trusted to make regular payments, on time. That ability makes up about 1/3 of your credit score, so take it seriously. A secured credit card is another option, which basically works the same way as a secured loan from your bank.

As a final option you can be added as an 'authorized user' on someone else's credit card but obviously that may be harder to do because there is no incentive for the other person to add you but maybe your parents or siblings will. Just make sure you know they pay on time because if not, you get hit with a drop in your credit score just as they do.

35% of your score is derived from payment history and missing even a single payment can result in a 50 to 100 point drop in your score, depending on several factors. Another 30% of your credit score is derived from your "debt burden", which is the amount of your outstanding balance compared to how much credit you have total. In other words, if you have 3 credit cards with $1,000 limits on each one for a total of $3,000 of credit and you maintain a balance on any or all of them that totals, say, $500 it can bring down your score. The higher the balance, the more it hurts your score. This is also why it can lower your score if you close credit accounts because you're effectively lowering the amount of credit you have, thus raising the debt-to-credit ratio. For example, if you have 3 credit cards with $1,000 limits on each one, keep an outstanding balance of $500 on one (or two or three) card, your debt-to-credit ratio is 16.7% (500 divided by 3000). If you close one card, now you only have $2,000 in credit total. Your debt-to-credit ratio is now 25% (500 divided by 2000). Credit scores are very sensitive so if you have credit cards, or any other credit extended to you, be very careful about how you manage them and make sure you always pay on time.

School Loans

Another gateway into massive amounts of debt is school loans. However, school loans are a necessary evil. Or are they?

If you were born after 1985, likely you've come to realize that bachelor's degrees have almost become relegated to the level of a high school diploma - you won't even get a toe in the door without one. There is so much greater access to schooling after high school now it's become almost strange to *not* have at least some college under a person's belt. Not too long ago, likely when your parents were growing up, a college degree was "a rich people thing". Going to college was a very well respected, privileged-only pursuit in life and if you actually finished with a degree, the world was your oyster. The next step was to get an entry-level career job in your field, work 30 years, retire with a gold watch, and live out the rest of your days on the beach of some tropical utopia.

Long gone are those days.

Now, it seems, *everyone* has a bachelor's degree and half of everyone has a master's. "Entry-level" job ads practically require some college these days. When I say entry-level here, I mean cashier at the supermarket. (No offense to any cashiers, I was a cashier in at least 3 jobs. I know the struggle). I have seen dozens of job ads for a simple Data Entry role requiring a college degree. As if anyone from the US under the age of 35 needs a degree to use a computer.

In the age of Millennials, the power of the internet and smart phones, the age of app-based startups like Uber, AirBNB, Snapchat, and WhatsApp, college and degrees are fast becoming obsolete. I don't want to get too far ahead of myself here but I want to bring your attention to the environment in which we live these days.

We don't graduate college and get hired in a career level job anymore. We move back in with parents and work low-paying hourly jobs. We don't stay at one career for 30 years and retire. We job hop. We are following in our parents' footsteps less and less and instead crafting our own worlds and side hustles through curiosity and innovation and youthful, clever ideas backed by the technology of our time. The requirement for higher education is slipping further and further into the background, in a sense.

I think it's a good thing, honestly. You don't need to go to a big university anymore to get a world-class education and become something. You have the internet. You have the ability to explore literally and absolutely *anything you want to* right at your finger tips. You can become a master in art and use Instagram to share your work with the world. Maybe you're a virtuoso who spreads the gift of music via Soundcloud. Maybe you want to become an international superstar through a YouTube channel.

The point I'm trying to make here to you is that going to school is still a very respectable, admirable thing to pursue in your life. It took me 7 years to get my 4-year bachelor's, but I got it. It's an achievement. But achieving goals, creating your dreams, getting that perfect job does not require you to go into debt that you will virtually never escape from. If you can afford to pay your way through school, do it – absolutely. If you can get a full scholarship, do it. If you can receive government aid, do it. Take full advantage of the resources afforded to you. Just do it sensibly, do it with your financial goals and your budget in mind.

Amanda Reaume, creator of *Millennial Personal Finance*, a blog that discusses various aspects of finance for millennials, describes her experience of a few sleepless nights trying to figure out how she would ever be able to pay for her own college because her parents were not able to cover all of the costs.

Reaume not only found a way to pay for her entire Master's degree in full, but came out on the other end of her graduate program with absolutely no debt, her degree attained in just 4 years, a job, and had $40,000 in the bank. How did she manage such a feat?

She explains that there were two main keys in her endeavor to finance her formal educational goals. The first is that she lived on a very tight budget and lived within her means. "While I wasn't able to live at home to save money, another easy way to live frugally is to learn to cook." Notice the strategy of cutting spending here. "I was able to save significant amounts of money by developing a strict budget and adhering to it", says Reaume. "I was less tempted to spend money on clothes or going out for expensive dinners when I had a clear idea of how much I could spend every month."

The second key to Reaume's feat, as she describes being the biggest difference, was that she won scholarships – $60,000 in total, to be exact. "So many students think that they can't win scholarships, but the truth is that there are scholarships out there for everyone. You just need to learn how to find, prioritize, and apply for scholarships", she says.

Clearly, Reaume exemplifies what is possible for a young person seeking higher education, if they are smart about it and take advantage of resources available to them, other than financial aid (remember effectuation, act based on what you have available now). Many people, however, may not have access to the same resources. But that is no reason to approach education with the mindset that a) you must go to college to get an education and b) you will need financial aid to do so. Just promise yourself that you will not bury yourself under a mountain of debt that you won't be able to pay down over your life time.

It will not likely be worth it.

Auto Loans

I think by now, even though it is still early, you're beginning to understand how to manage money better and the overall message I'm trying to deliver to you. But I want to take another brief moment to address auto loans and how to approach them because, let's face it, you almost have to have a car to live anywhere in this country. The exception is if you live in a large, metropolitan city with well-developed mass transit and maybe a couple other exceptions but the majority of you, I'm sure, have a car, truck, or motorcycle.

I already mentioned the wisest approach to owning an asset and that is to own it outright. Pay in full. But if you are going to actually finance a vehicle, do some research. Find out the costs of owning the vehicle, long-term. There are online calculators that can give estimates on the true cost of owning whatever car you probably want to buy. They cover things like the wear and tear based on your expected mileage each year, the maintenance the car will probably need, and other various costs of owning your car of choice. Make sure you do not pay MSRP pricing either as this "sticker price" is usually marked up substantially by the dealer.

When you finance, do your best to get the lowest monthly payment while still making efforts to pay it off quickly. The interest rate on the loan has a strong impact on the amount of your payment, as does the length of time you agree to on the loan (terms are usually 36, 48, 60, or 72 months). 4% interest versus 10% interest makes almost a $100 difference in your monthly payment on a $25,000 note. Also, your credit score will be a big factor in determining your interest rate, so the better your credit, the lower your interest rate. Bring the biggest down payment that you can because a down payment (immediate equity in the car you're buying and seen as a good-faith payment) knocks down the total amount of the loan you are applying for and thus you pay it off faster. Remember, you want to pay in full as much as you can so you can pay it off sooner and avoid unnecessary payment on the interest of the loan. A car that costs $15,000, when financed for 60 months at 5% interest (great credit), costs you an extra $1,900 in interest payments. At 10% interest, it's about $4,000.

You may not know this, but a car is the worst asset you can buy, financially speaking. This is because as soon as you drive the car off the dealership lot, it very literally loses its value. In fact, to take it a step beyond, it's even worse because this particular big ticket item doesn't return you even $1 of profit.

Ok, the exception is if you keep the car long enough and eventually it becomes considered a "classic" or an "antique". Then it can gain back value. But realistically, it's very unlikely your car will reach that status for several reasons.

All that being said, buy a car you can afford. Not a car you simply want. Buying a car you just want because of the way it looks or the way it makes you feel or you thinking it helps your status, is entirely ego-based. Basing your financial decisions, and thus your well-being, on your ego is suicide. Buy a car you can afford, one that fits your budget and won't have you sleepless at night because you don't if your car will be in the driveway in the morning or on the back of a tow truck because you're behind 3 payments.

Avoid Debt

I hope you have understood the general idea over these last few sections on debt and that it is becoming clearer to you how to better control your spending, manage your finances, and live within your means. These things are crucial to your financial health and even your physical health because stress and unhappiness can quite literally age you and eventually end your life earlier than it would otherwise.

I don't mean to be morbid. I want to impart to you the knowledge and wisdom and experience I've gained in my short time on this planet in a way that is impactful and objective. Debt is a very real threat. Not just to you but even mega corporations across the globe. Every economic "bubble" (the thing that, when it pops, causes major economic recessions, job loss, turmoil, social and political unrest, and trillions of dollars lost around the world) we have ever had in history has been rooted in debt that cannot be paid back.

Don't get into debt and become overwhelmed trying to stay afloat. Avoid it all together.

You now understand the third step to financial management. Avoid debt.

PART II: Deploying Your Money

To this point, I have primarily discussed gaining control of your money and building it into a real asset. By now you should have a much better understanding of where you are financially, how to think about your money and the approach to managing it, and several methods to better control it. The strategy in Part I was making smart decisions to control your money.

Now you need to know how to deploy it in a way that will move you toward your goals faster and in a protected manner. The strategy here will be making smart decisions to *grow and protect* your money.

Chapter 4: Invest

"Your job does not determine your wealth or success. What you do with your income does." –
James Sackey

What to Invest In

There are literally hundreds of different ways to invest money in our world and tens of thousands of companies that are publically traded right here in America. Dozens upon dozens of investment vehicles exist with an infinite range of possibilities and outcomes and returns or losses. Of course, there are also dozens of books that have been written on the subject and concepts put into practice on investing, even as far back as Babylon (about 3900 years ago).

There is virtually an endless abyss of opportunities, hundreds of so-called gurus hawking their system or product, relentless bombardment from news media, friends, and family. It is staggering the amount of "investments" that can come your way over a lifetime. But it needn't be so convoluted. There really are only maybe a handful of places the average person should park their money and it depends on a few factors: your age, your income, and overall financial position such as the amount of savings, debt, and assets you have as well as what kind of other obligations you may have like a spouse or children.

However, I must advise ultimately that you steer very clear of the super-majority of "opportunities" that come your way – they will undoubtedly be fraught with perils and pitfalls only to see you lose your precious army of hard-earned dollars. Investments are even more dangerous than credit cards because with credit cards at least you know what you're getting yourself into. I'm an expert in finance and investing money and I have lost plenty of money. Anyone who invests money loses at one point or another. The trick is losing as little as possible. For you though, stay away.

There are really only two areas to invest your money: in the broad financial market or in your own field/business.

How to Invest

The broad financial market refers to the stock market, at least in this book. But be careful here. You should not be choosing individual stocks or going off some recommendation from a close friend or some pundit's pick of the week or the new fad to invest in (think, bitcoin). Forsake all of them. You need to be broad in your investment into financial markets. It is the best way to ensure the risks posed are minimized – even though there are still many risks. The best way to do that is through buying what is called an Exchange-Traded Fund, or ETF.

ETFs are essentially a basket of securities ("securities" means any of the following: stocks like Amazon or Starbucks, bonds like government bonds, commodities like gold and oil, or even currencies like dollars or yen, etc.). "Basket" means like a bunch of stocks or a bunch of commodities grouped into one. Think of it like buying a car dealership. There are many cars within the dealership, several different models and trims, each with their own value that goes up and down. But you bought the *dealership*, with all the cars in it, for a single price. That single price was derived from the value of *all* of those individual cars, rolled into one price. That's basically how an ETF works. For a single price, you buy the one asset that houses several other assets in it and the value of your single asset comes from the values of the individuals within it.

There are several different types of ETFs available to you as well. Such as stock ETFs, which hold groups of different stocks like blue chip companies you've probably heard of like Apple, Wal-Mart, Ford, and GE, to name a few. There are bond ETFs which hold different bonds, sometimes with varying maturities like 2, 5, or 10 years or longer. There are gold ETFs which hold various gold-mining company stocks or gold distributors. There are even ETFs that represent entire countries or regions such as the US as a single country or all of Europe like France, Germany, England, and Italy. An ETF usually holds 100 different individual securities within it thereby representing a broad, diversified investment vehicle.

Investing in an ETF is also part of a strategy known as indexing (or "passive" investing), which means the ETF tracks the value of an underlying security or securities. So a US market ETF tracks the value of several US-based companies that trade on some US stock exchange. A regional ETF, such as a BRIC ETF ("BRIC" stands for Brazil, Russia, India, China, or basically "developing countries") would track several large and prominent companies that operate in a region or in each of those countries. So maybe something like, 10 large companies in different industries based in Russia, 40 companies based in Brazil, 50 companies based in India, and another 50 companies based in China. Your money would be spread across several countries, or companies or bonds, or wherever. It keeps your money relatively safe as it's never concentrated in one place.

This will be your bread and butter method of investing. The majority of people should invest their money in this manner whether it is their savings or retirement cash. It is also cost-effective as ETFs are very low-cost (remember compounding interest and how it can add up dramatically over time) and they're tax friendly – you can buy this type of investment vehicle in your retirement accounts. This is the method of investing that two legendary investors, Warren Buffett and Jack Bogle, recommend for the average investor. Unless there needs to be some exception like the following scenario or any other scenario, this is the only method or strategy that need be applied in your investing of money.

Your other option is to invest your money into your chosen field or your business, which may be one in the same but not necessarily. A chosen field might be the medical field in which you're pursuing a career as a physician of some kind. In that case, you would probably want to invest your money in all of the necessary education required to become a physician and then beyond that in your own continuing education and self-development.

An actual business you create would be something like your own restaurant or clothing storefront for example. In which case, the rule of thumb from the greatest business owners and managers of all-time apply the same philosophy: reinvest all of your earnings back into your business, rinse, and repeat.

Either way, if you have decided to walk the path of some form of entrepreneurship, then you will want to invest every bit of your money into that path. In fact, you will *need* to invest it all and then some because the path of the entrepreneur is intensive; labor intensive, capital intensive, emotionally intensive, and everything in between.

My suggestion then on how to invest in your own career path is to invest in as much education, training, and development as possible. Let me say that again, *as much as possible*. That is what it will take to become successful, I promise you that. Personal development and training will not only define you but will make or break your endeavor.

Investment Management

Managing your investments is relatively easy and straightforward. You simply continue doing what you're doing from start to finish. Remember the power of habit and compounding. Over time, your investments will become massive and fruitful. Continuously invest your money into your retirement and brokerage (investing) accounts, into your chosen ETF(s), as religiously as you pay your bills.

For how long? Years. Decades. Forever. Until you retire.

Continuously invest in your business and professional self-development. For how long? Years. Decades. Forever. Until you retire.

The beginning will be slow. It is true. It will feel like nothing is happening or the money and returns are too small and insignificant. That is purely inexperience or your ego feeding you falsehoods. Rein it in and decide that what you're doing is the right way and that it will pay off in the end because it will. All big and great things take a long time and a whole lot of consistency.

The most successful know this.

They know that to be truly successful and build anything of great value, one must walk the path continuously, relentlessly, and all the way to the end, regardless of distractions or mistakes or pitfalls or naysayers, and only then will the reward come.

Money adds up. Time afforded adds up. Development, training, and education adds up. You know this. Do it.

You now understand the fourth step in financial management. Invest.

Chapter 5: Insurance

"The extent of the struggle determines the extent of the growth." – Ryan Holiday

Insurance is probably the least understand area of personal finance yet one of the most important because it involves protecting all the things that are valuable in your life – including yourself. You need to protect everything you've worked for, even if you don't believe that you have many valuable things to protect. But if you took inventory of everything you own, you would probably be surprised. Your car, clothing, your electronics, books, furniture, can all add up rather quickly. Especially when you add your most valuable asset: you and your earning ability. For that reason, we now turn to protecting your assets.

Before we get into some of the details, I want to give a brief overview of insurance and some of the best practices for you to pick up so you're using your dollars most effectively. However, given the aim of the book, I won't go into great detail on some of the smaller aspects of insurance such as possible discounts, from whom exactly to buy insurance, and the like. Once you begin looking to cover yourself through insurance, most of these smaller details will come to your attention either through the dealer you buy from or your own research.

There are some broad and important practices to use when buying insurance. It is meant to protect you from a financial catastrophe. It is not to protect you from small bumps in your life like getting into a fender bender because you were driving while texting when you should have been watching the car ahead of you. Financial catastrophe is when you experience such a major event that is not only extremely expensive to pay for but also sets you back so far financially that it will probably take several months or years to get out of a very deep financial hole. We're talking tens or hundreds of thousands of dollars. Keep in mind too, when it comes to rising medical costs, severe illness can easily run into the million dollar range when you need to receive treatments that are less common than your average flu medicine.

In 2014, a young woman of the age of 25, an up-and-coming comedian, thought insurance wasn't exactly a priority at the time because she was having trouble making ends meet (sound like someone we know?). One day, she happened to faint on the platform of the subway. What she miraculously awoke to was nothing short of a nightmare. She had fallen onto the tracks and was run over by a train. She obviously survived. But needless to say, the costs of saving her life were very high; $405,000.

These situations can ruin you financially for a very, very long time. Not to mention the emotional suffering you will most likely endure, which only adds to your health risks.

What if you have your own business? You're likely aware of some of the ridiculous claims people have been able to make over the years. Like the woman some years ago who sued Mcdonald's – *and won* – because she burned herself after spilling her coffee. After filing suit, the woman actually received a $640,000 payday. That was definitely the most expensive cup of coffee McDonald's has ever had to pay for – and it was *their* coffee.

Could *you* bounce back from these kinds of situations? Not likely. That is why it is so important to protect yourself and your assets. That being said, I want to cover a few important aspects of insurance and how to address them.

Three Rules of Insurance

The first rule is this: buy insurance for the big stuff and ignore the small stuff. Remember, insurance is meant to cover financial catastrophe, not missing your flight to Hawaii. Your insurance policy should always seek to cover big ticket items. There are really 3 major things you need to protect and they are your income earning ability – what life and long-term disability insurance protect; your health – what health insurance is for; and then any businesses you might own – which is what liability insurance is for.

The next rule is to buy broad coverage. You want to buy an insurance policy that will cover a wide range of events that may occur in your life so that you don't risk a lack of coverage due to some technical gap in your policy. For example, something like buying homeowners' insurance will cover any normal loss of your home, like if a fire burns your house to the ground. But your insurance might not cover earthquake damages because sometimes that kind of coverage is a separate feature, more so in areas where it is less common.

Finally, you need to make sure that when you buy insurance you shop around and buy directly from the insurer. You want to avoid buying from an agent (broker), if you can. They typically make buying insurance much more expensive due to commissions and the conflict of interest due to their income being based on what they sell you. Insurance agents are known for pitching insurance policies and extra cost features that are either unnecessary or overkill. Remember how small things compound over time. These extra dollars in your premium add up.

Health Insurance

Health insurance is the most important type of insurance because it's the one that practically everyone needs to have and is probably the most frequently used (or at least should be the most frequently used). Health insurance is meant to cover the expenses of medical care in the event that you're in an accident, you become affected by some illness or disease, or you simply need to go to the doctor for a prescription.

You are the most important thing in your life. You are an asset. So your health is the first grounds where you protect this asset. Remember, again, the effects of compounding. To ensure your health through the coming decades and into a long retirement where you can enjoy the fruits of your following the principals in this book, you must take the necessary actions to stay healthy. That means going to the doctor when you get sick, getting regular check-ups, taking medication when the situation calls for it. This is how you catch early onsets of ailments and diseases that may be stopped before they really begin to affect you. Be proactive.

As far as going about buying health insurance, all you really have to do is adhere to the 3 rules I outlined previously. You need to buy for the big stuff. For health insurance, that means buying comprehensive insurance. In other words, major medical insurance that covers things like x-rays, prescription costs, hospital stays, it covers women who may want to have kids, and most other situations that would otherwise cost you thousands of dollars, if not more.

Buying broad coverage is important again. You need to be sure that you understand what exactly your health insurance plan will pay for prior to you needing it. Sometimes child birth or certain drugs are not included in insurance plans. You also want to consider your choice of healthcare provider. They are two main choices: health maintenance organizations (HMOs) and preferred provider organizations (PPOs). These plans restrict your choices but they are typically less costly because they negotiate lower rates with selected providers. The main difference between the two types of providers is that PPOs will usually still pay the majority of your medical expenses if you go to a physician outside of their approved list. HMOs, however, will not typically cover any of your expenses if you go outside of their providers.

Another feature to consider in your health insurance plan is the lifetime maximum benefits. This is the maximum amount your plan will pay out over the life of your policy and could top out too quickly should you ever come down with a severe illness or major accident and need expensive treatment. Ideally, you want to buy a policy with no maximum or one that has at least a $5 million maximum. Also, make sure to buy a policy that comes with a *guaranteed renewability* feature. This ensures that when your policy expires, you can renew it without having to go through a medical evaluation that may determine you have a new condition, thus rendering you uninsurable. Features like this are known as "riders". Be careful with riders though because they can get out of hand quickly and end up costing you a lot more than is necessary.

Disability Insurance

The next major insurance protection you should probably invest in is disability insurance. This is meant to protect the ability to earn an income for yourself – the 2nd most important asset after your own health.

First you need to decide whether you need to get coverage. There are some exceptions to whether or not you need disability insurance because of what it protects. For example, if you're married and your spouse makes enough money to support the both of you without any change in your lifestyle, you may not necessarily need to buy disability insurance. But that is a risky proposition as most people cannot live without their employment income and, of course, things can change unexpectedly during your life.

Don't think you're invincible either. It's easy to dismiss disability coverage because we constantly think, "that won't happen to me" or "the odds of that are slim" More than 33% of disabilities are suffered by people under 45 years old. Again, be proactive.

Figuring out the amount of disability insurance you need is not particularly difficult. It is meant to cover your income. Which means if you became disabled and could no longer work, your disability insurance replaces your after-tax income. So if your employment income is $4,500 a month, after taxes, your disability insurance benefit should be $4,500 a month.

Disability benefits are tax-free, so you don't need to calculate that into it. Also, you'll want your benefits to run all the way to the age that you retire at, like age 65 when Social Security kicks in. While there are several features you need to investigate when buying this type of insurance, such as *guaranteed renewability* again, there's one in particular I will suggest. It is a Cost-of-Living Adjustments (COLAs) feature. It basically adjusts your benefits according to inflation. This will ensure that your benefits retain their purchasing power through any fluctuations in the cost of living. As usual, avoid purchasing through an agent as that conflict of interest and urge to sell you high-end products can end up costing you much more in premiums.

Life Insurance

The final piece of major insurance on you is life insurance. This kind of policy is a little less of a requirement only because there are several exceptions of people who don't need it.

These are people who are:
- Single with no kids
- Couples that could maintain their lifestyle on only one of their incomes
- Wealthy
- Minors
- Retired people living on their nest egg

If you have anyone who is dependent on your paycheck, you need to have life insurance as it covers all of the income you would have made had you not passed away – it replaces your life's income, in effect. If you have dependents and you were to die during your primary earning years, life insurance provides a lump sum payment that can ensure your benefits go to pay all or part of the large expenses that you may have outstanding such as your mortgage, college for your kids, or any other big ticket items you wouldn't want to burden your family with paying.

Figuring out how much life insurance you need to buy is fairly straight-forward – a nice gift in the world of insurance. Essentially, all you need to do is calculate how much money you would need to replace (your after-tax income) from now till the time you plan to retire.

Another way to calculate how much life insurance you need is to think about how much you'll need to pay for the big ticket items you owe money on. Take all the debts you want the policy to pay off, add them up, and buy that amount of life insurance.

Remember that this book is not intended to be a full-fledged, comprehensive course in personal finance. It is intended to address the biggest areas of your finances. That being said, make sure to do your research and maybe at least consult with (not necessarily hire) insurance and tax professionals to get a more in-depth review of some of these areas of your financial health. Everyone's situation is unique.

Now I need to address the two main types of life insurance: *term* and *cash value*. Let me say this now to get it out of the way; you need to buy term life insurance.

Cash value life insurance has a few different names and variations such as whole, universal, and variable.

Regardless of the variation, skip it!

Cash value life insurance is expensive to the highest fault. Anyone who says otherwise is either ill-advised or an agent trying to sell you. The only exception *might* be if you're a wealthy individual with a big business. Even then, you likely don't really need a cash value life insurance policy. (The reason there may be an exception is for estate tax purposes for those who are wealthy but, as usual, there are alternatives that yield the same results for less cost.) To give you an idea of the cost difference between cash value and term life insurance, some sources report cash value policies costing as much as 8x more than a term policy, with no real added value. Enough said.

Term life insurance is pure life insurance. You pay an annual premium and receive coverage in a specified amount that pays out to your beneficiaries in the event that you die. Nothing could be simpler in explanation. I won't use up your time to explain all the bunk information or outright lies an agent might use to try and sell you on a cash value policy. Just know not to buy. It will waste very valuable dollars in the long run (and short run).

There are really only a few items I will address in terms of life insurance that you need to make sure are a part of your policy. The first main item is that you can select how often your premium adjusts. The premium adjusts upward (assuming you renew) because as you get older, the risk of you dying increases and insurance companies need to offset their risk in insuring your life. Typically, the length of a policy is 5, 10, 15, and 20 years but you can get further out if you desire.

You may be thinking, "OK, I'll just go for the longest length so my premium doesn't adjust". Not so fast speed racer. The disadvantage of locking in your rate for a long time is that you pay more in the early years than you do on a policy that adjusts more frequently. Don't get confused here; your premium doesn't change *during* the length of your policy. What "pay more in the early years" means is that, because you chose a long-term policy, your premium is going to be higher throughout the length of the policy as opposed to if you had just chosen something like a 5-year length. In other words, a 5-year policy might cost you $30 a month in premiums versus a 20-year policy that costs you $40. Keep in mind, you want to control and be efficient with your money. Compounding is at play again here (it always is). You can save the difference in policy premiums and invest them. Think long-term

Also, when you go to renew your policy, if you chose a longer length of time, the upward jump in your premium is higher – yet again costing you more at the onset of your coverage. For these reasons, a happy medium is a 5 to 10 year policy.

Another item to address, as in disability and health insurance, is the *guaranteed renewability* feature. Make sure your policy comes with this. You don't want to have a solid policy expire on you and then you can't renew because your health conditions have changed, unless of course you believe your life insurance needs disappear at the end of your policy's term (it only needs to cover you up to retirement).

Finally, as with the last two forms of insurance discussed, avoid buying from an agent and shop around and buy direct.

Other Assets

Now that we've discussed insuring yourself, we turn to insuring everything else that is important in your life: all of your prized possessions. No, not your pokemon cards from high school. That would be small potatoes, right? And we only buy insurance for the big stuff.

The big ticket items are your home or apartment, your car, and yes, actually, your personal belongings – not individual items though. Let's start with your home.

Dwelling coverage is definitely something you want to have if you're a homeowner. This type of insurance protects you from the costs of having to rebuild your home based on the square footage, not the value of the home or the size of your mortgage. If you're a renter, you don't need to buy dwelling insurance. With your homeowners' insurance you want to make sure you buy a policy that has a *guaranteed replacement cost* provision. That way, you can make sure that the insurance company will pay for the costs to rebuild the home even if the cost of construction exceeds the insurance policy's coverage.

Your personal belongings can be insured as well. As I mentioned though before, you want insurance for all of your things under one policy, not each individual item – remember the rule, broad coverage. The amount of coverage you can get for your things is usually calculated as a percentage of your homeowners' insurance policy. Typically, this amount is around 50% of your dwelling coverage, which is usually more than enough.

If you have belongings that are big ticket items, like large amounts of expensive jewelry that you think might exceed the amount of insurance you're covered for, you might consider some kind of rider on your policy. But more than likely, you do not need this or any other type of rider. Don't be sold on added bells and whistles.

As a renter, you need to calculate the amounts of everything of value that you own so that you can figure out how much insurance to buy. Like I said before, the total value of your things will probably surprise you.

A final note on property insurance, if you live in an area that is prone to earthquakes, floods, mudslides or the like, make sure that whatever policy you decide to buy covers damages from these disasters. There are not usually included in the policy, even if it's a comprehensive one. Insurance companies are trying to mitigate the risk of having to payout insurance claims. Ensure there are no unexpected gaps in your protection. Yes, it *can* happen to you. At the time of this writing, Texas, Florida, islands in the Caribbean and several other areas located around the Gulf of Mexico are dealing with the damages of Hurricane Harvey (the 3rd costliest Atlantic hurricane) and Irma (a category 5 hurricane with winds up to 185MPH). Harvey has caused upwards of $70 billion worth of damage, primarily to residents and businesses of Houston, TX. Irma caused an estimated $63 billion+. I have a friend that lives in Tampa Bay preparing for the storm to hit. But I'm betting she and her family are not fully insured for the damages that could very well occur as a result of the storm.

Auto Insurance

Now we move on to the final asset you absolutely need to have insurance on: your car. This should go without saying, but driving without insurance is not only against the law but a huge financial vulnerability as vehicle repair costs can run up very quickly and legal penalties if you're involved in an accident with another driver are stiff.

At the very least, you should be carrying bodily injury/property damage liability insurance, or simply *liability* insurance. This covers any damages on another person or any property that you cause with your vehicle (or a rented vehicle).

If I haven't incentivized you enough already on this type of insurance, let me also explain to you that should you be involved in an accident and you're not covered with liability insurance, you can be sued. Lawsuits can garnish your future income. Do not let that happen. It will never be worth the risk.

On the flip side, should you be in an accident that was not your fault and the other driver is uninsured or *under*insured, there is something called *uninsured or underinsured motorist liability coverage* that allows you to collect for lost wages, medical expenses, and pain and suffering. However, if you already have comprehensive health insurance and disability insurance, you don't really need this extra coverage. The only disadvantage in this though is that without uninsured or underinsured liability coverage, you lose the ability to sue for pain and suffering, as well as any coverage for passengers riding with you that are not covered by their own insurance.

Wills

On one final note about protection, let me inform you on a will and how it works, as well as a couple other features of a will. A will is basically a set of instructions on how to distribute all your worldly possessions after you die. If you have kids, a will is a necessity. This is because your heirs are powerless in regards to your possessions and assets upon your death and a court in the state you live in will decide what happens to your things. It can be a lengthy and costly process as well. You don't want a court deciding who will raise your kids and where your money will go.

There are two things you can add to your will and that is a *living* will and *medical power of attorney.* A living will tells your doctor what life-support measures you prefer, if any. For example, if you're in a coma, you obviously can't speak. Who speaks for you? Your living will does (because you're not technically dead yet). Medical power of attorney grants authority to someone you trust to make decisions on your medical care options if, for some reason, you're unable to do so yourself.

Setting these up is not particularly difficult but if you find it overwhelming, consult an attorney to help you. You do not *need* to hire an attorney for these things. It can be costly to do so, as always with hiring professionals. There are plenty of simple online methods of getting a will, a living will, and medical power of attorney with it.

You now understand the fifth step in financial management. Protect your assets.

Conclusion: Pulling It All Together

"The empires of the future are the empires of the mind." – Winston Churchill

You have made it to the end of the book. Now that you have, how do you feel? My hope is that you feel more empowered, knowledgeable, capable, and informed on just what it means to be financially healthy and with some solid know-how when it comes to managing your finances. I hope that I have imparted enough of my experience, knowledge, and insight to you so that you can now go forward knowing that you will be better at managing your money and that you will retire with a healthy nest-egg that is fully protected against many unexpected events.

I can only hope that you have grasped the concepts in this book enough to understand that all of it matters, all of it counts, it is all important to your financial health and your well-being. You should now understand the power of compounding and habit and how all of the things you do every single day add up in the end. That every single dollar you save or spend adds up and compounds on itself. You should understand that managing your money well enough to retire isn't very hard to do if you are willing to save consistently, sacrifice a few luxuries in your life now in exchange for a future payoff, and live within your means and adhere to the five steps I have outlined: save your money regularly; use a budget and live within your means; avoid getting into debt; invest your money; and protect your assets. These are all logical, sensible things to do but in their simplicity and lack of presence within traditional educational programs, they have almost become esoteric – reserved for the elite, the privileged, and the well-connected.

We have to change that.

Share what you have learned. Share this book, if you can. Pass-on knowledge. I am a firm believer in openly sharing information, expertise, and insight, especially if it is beneficial to many people and to the betterment of life in general. That is a very personal and ultimate goal of mine – bettering other people's lives. Please help me achieve it by sharing what I have expounded upon with you in this book.

Knowledge of, skill, wisdom, and experience with money is something to be shared and taught. Whenever possible. If someone is willing to listen, learn, apply, develop, or grow, there is absolutely no reason to withhold information.

I will leave you with a quote I once heard that struck me and I remind myself of often, in regards to the self and perception of self and others. "There's no nobility in being superior to your fellow man. Nobility is being superior to your former self." – Unknown

Books to Read

As an avid reader, I thought it necessary to suggest some good reading to those who appreciate a good book. My favorite subjects are finance and business (if that wasn't obvious), psychology/sociology, and war and strategy. There are many more but these are some of my favorite and the most influential books I have read.

The Richest Man In Babylon by George S. Clason

The Little Book Of Common Sense Investing by John C. Bogle

Elements of Investing by Burton Malkiel and Charles Ellis

The Intelligent Investor by Benjamin Graham

Focus: The Hidden Driver of Excellence by Daniel Goleman

How Rich People Think by Steven Siebold

Rich Habits by Thomas Corely

The One Thing by Gary Keller

Think and Grow Rich by Napoleon Hill

The Obstacle Is The Way by Ryan Holiday

Ego Is The Enemy by Ryan Holiday

Common Stocks and Uncommon Profits by Phillip Fischer

Art of War by Sun Tzu

The Book of Five Rings by Miyamoto Musashi

Connecting With Me

If you would like to connect with me, I am very active online and on some social media. You can connect with me via www.boardwalkave.wordpress.com , my blog that focuses on money and investing. I'm also active on LinkedIn, www.linkedin.com/in/jamessackey as well as Twitter @TheBoardwalkAve and Pinterest. I also write for www.Investing.com. Otherwise you can reach me at sackeyjames@gmail.com If you have any questions, insights or experiences to share, comments or feedback to make, please, feel free to drop a line. I love feedback.

www.ingramcontent.com/pod-product-compliance
Lightning Source LLC
Chambersburg PA
CBHW070316230526
45470CB00002B/897